PIANO

DR. JOHN
TEACHES
New Orleans Piano
VOL. 3
Sanctifying the Blues

Cover Photo by Chris Rials-Seitz

Audio Editors: George James and Ted Orr

Mastered by: Ted Orr at
Nevessa Productions, Woodstock, NY

Produced by Happy Traum for Homespun Tapes

ISBN 0-7935-8178-8

EXCLUSIVELY DISTRIBUTED BY

HAL•LEONARD®
CORPORATION
7777 W. BLUEMOUND RD. P.O. BOX 13819 MILWAUKEE, WI 53213

© 1997 HOMESPUN TAPES LTD.
BOX 694
WOODSTOCK, NY 12498-0694
All Rights Reserved

No part of this publication may be reproduced in any form or by any means
without the prior written permission of the Publisher.

Visit Hal Leonard Online at **www.halleonard.com**

Visit Homespun Tapes on the internet at **http://www.homespuntapes.com**

CD instruction makes it easy! Find the section of the lesson you want with the press of a finger; play that segment over and over until you've mastered it; easily skip over parts you've already mastered—no clumsy rewinding or fast-forwarding to find your spot; listen with the best possible audio fidelity; follow along track-by-track with the book.

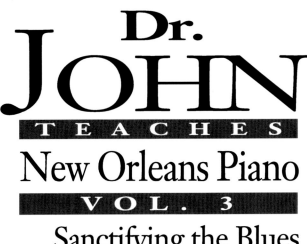

Table of Contents

Church

◆❶ Introduction–About Church Music

This is Dr. John the Night Tripper, and one of the things that I think is very important to all of this is that the blues came from the church. And you can't get away from the church music sound.

◆❷ Song for Mother

This is a song in 6/8, or 12/8 or 3/4 even, which was written for my mother. It's very churchy and will give you an idea of the church music sound.

Song For Mother

That sound is very indicative of the sanctified church influence. It's important for people to understand how the church feeling is tied into *all* music, not just the blues. Church music does serve a higher purpose in bringing people together. I believe that you can't get away from the church roots, even if you were to play the most gut-bucket blues. If I play it long enough, some way it's going to run to where it feels churchy.

I'd say today that most blues singers, whether it's B.B. King or whoever, they like to sing with a church feeling because most singers have come out of the church. It's real important for people to know this.

◆ "Something You Got"

Take a song like "Something You Got," which was a rhythm-and-blues hit years ago.

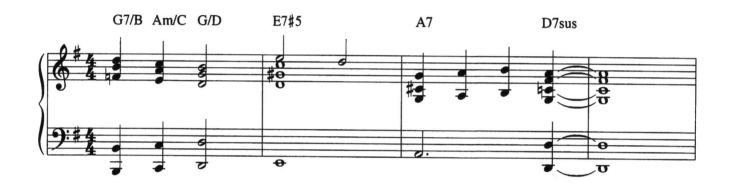

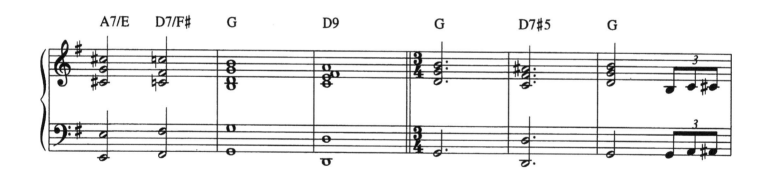

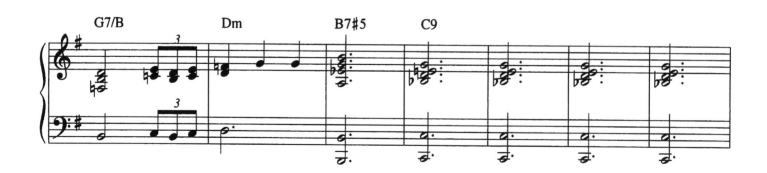

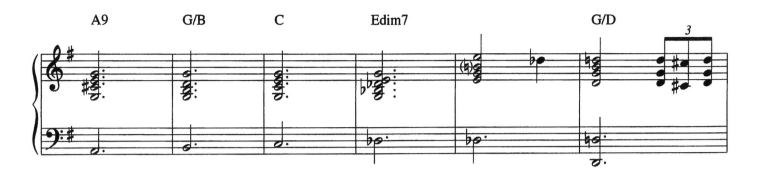

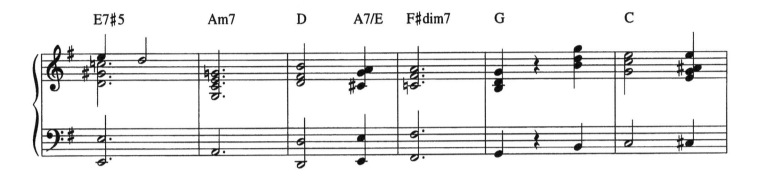

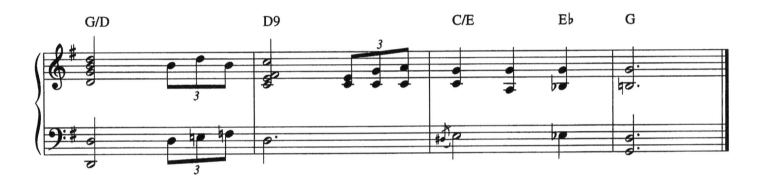

All of these songs have that definite church thing in them, like "Something You Got" or "Just A Closer Walk With Thee." You can't get away from it. As much as over the years the blues have been frowned on by the church people, and blues people have said that the church people were stuck up or whatever, the music is a uniting factor.

◆4 Gospel Analysis

In gospel music, we use a lot of thirds in the bass and real basic triads.

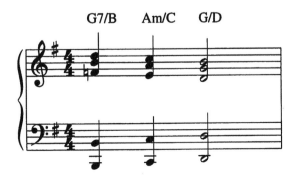

And in the VI chord in this example, the fifth is raised or augmented,

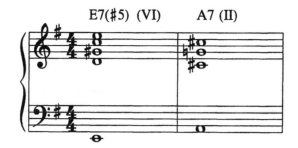

which resolves to the II chord.

We get to the V chord,

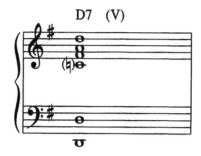

which resolves to II and then to V again.

Using an augmented chord for a V chord is very important.

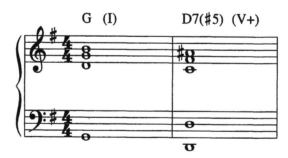

And the III chord going to the IV chord.

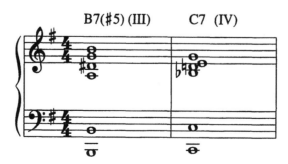

And a motion of chords from the major II chord leading to a diminished chord on the raised IV.

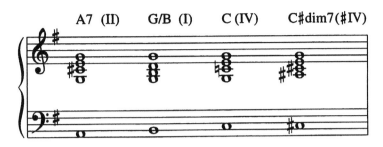

And, of course, the "Amen" ending.

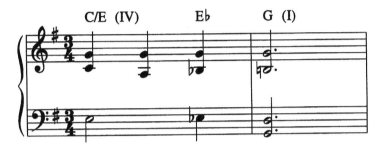

Those are basic elements of the church sound.

◆5 Gospel Rhythm

But the most important element of the church sound is to *feel* the song.

If it's a slow song in four, feel an underlying 6/8 or 12/8 triplet feel. It's very important to *feel* that. You can actually hear it on a lot of old records where there would be a tambourine playing:

It's a shuffle rhythm.

It's a locking point. When you have a big choir or it's just a soloist singing with that kind of rhythm under it, it leaves a whole lot of space for them to really embellish on a song properly.

⬥6 "Blueberry Hill"

This is in a lot of blues, where you hear the guys playing that Fats Domino "Blueberry Hill" style.

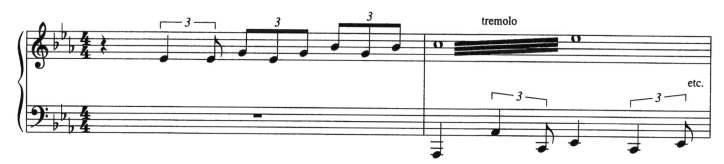

There's an underlying triplet rhythm, a 6/8 feeling.

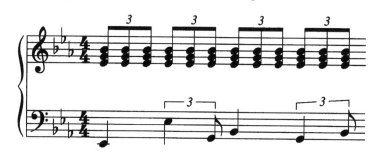

I've always found that in sanctified, spiritual churches that when they get a real good ballad with that rhythm going, it electrifies the church. It's something that always works, just as much as when they play the romping Baptist fast tunes.

⬥7 "Saints"

Here's an uptempo, "Holy Roller" type fast tune.

Saints

"Romp" Style

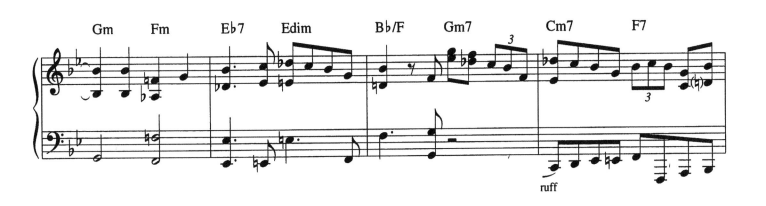

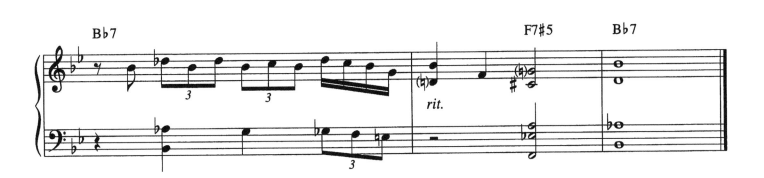

And this is the way we really play "Saints" in the church in New Orleans. It's slow and in a minor key.

When The Saints Go Marchin' In

Minor Blues Version

While we would play this, the little children would carry the candles up to the altar and it's a very beautiful thing. And after the candles are in place, that's when we would go into the romping version, that's much more well known.

We're using typical "churchy" chords.

Like they say, make a joyful noise unto the Lord and lift up your spirits. You can't beat that kind of music. Even at funerals when you hear the brass band playing a funeral dirge, when the dirge is over, they break into a song like "Didn't He Ramble" and it'll put you in a good mood. In New Orleans they picked up this thing that the Irish did at wakes, to keep a good set of vibes for the deceased to leave the planet on. You know—a joyful noise.

◆⑧ "When The Wicked Shall Cease"

When you hear the songs, like "When The Wicked Shall Cease," in the minor key, it's very somber.

When you hear the same melody in the major key ("Saints"), it all of a sudden has a totally different vibe.

◆⑨ Amens and Turnarounds

The church turnarounds vary from the blues turnarounds. In the church we play the real "Amen,"

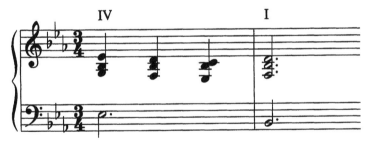

and there's so many ways to play the Amen, it's limitless. But in the blues, we use a turnaround.

Major/Minor
◆10 Major/Minor

The minor keys always set a more somber mood in the music. When you hear B.B. King sing "The Thrill Is Gone," the whole song is minor chords. There's not a single major chord in the song. And it works beautifully because of that. It keeps the song in a very somber mood throughout.

◆11 Charles Brown

Charles Brown will turn *within* a song from a minor to a major key very subtly and discreetly. He will do this even within a chord progression.

It just changes the mood ever so subtly when he slides from the minor to the major. And when he does the next section, he's in a major key. People hardly ever notice that it's changed, because it's not anything drastic.

◆12 Raised 9ths

I think a lot of the feel of the blues has to do with the usage of both minor and majors. In the blues, we have a lot of what we call raised 9 chords.

The Raised 9 Chord

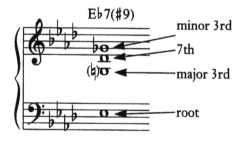

Raised 9 Chord Blues

That was a break song by many bands for years. It was the first song I remember Billy Butler would play on guitar raised 9 chords noticeably all the way through the song.

When you hear the raised 9 chord, it's neither major nor minor. It has the elements of a major chord because it has a major third, but it also has the minor third, so you have both. And this is important when you do blues songs, because in most songs the melody is on the minor third, even though the underlying chord may be major.

⑬ "Lonely Avenue"

⑭ 9ths Continued

"Lonely Avenue," recorded by Ray Charles, featured raised 9 chords throughout the song on all the changes. This opened the door for a lot of records later on, a lot of Memphis records or even the Beatles' "Sgt. Pepper," or "Shotgun." They all featured that raised 9 sound of the guitar.

Everything in music has a place and it has a use. It's just within people's tastes and what they can enjoy, whether they use it or whether they enjoy hearing it.

Blues/Gospel Link

⑮ Blues/Gospel Link

This is the area in which the blues and church music hits on the same thing, where people like Ray Charles and Aretha Franklin have done so well. I would recommend that you listen to their records, and Stevie Wonder's records, to get a full overview of how the blues are mixed with gospel. Take the early Ray Charles records like "Hallelujah." I love that. And when he did "Drown In My Own Tears." They are blues ballads, but are also church songs. If you change the lyrics to any one of them, they would be accepted in any church. These are secular songs that have been made real soulful and bluesy.

Even though Sam Cooke might have suffered for years when he crossed over the border from being a gospel singer to a pop singer, to me, Sam didn't sing any different when he became a pop singer that when he was a gospel singer, he just didn't have material as good. Because, a lot of the pop songs he ended up singing weren't of the caliber and soulfulness of, say, "Touch The Hem Of His Garment," which was the gospel record that most affected me. I remember in my youth when I first heard Sam Cooke sing "Touch the Hem Of His Garment" with the Soul Stirrers, there was nothing that I'd ever heard that touched me that way. The same thing happened a little later when I heard him sing some pop songs, too. It was an *experience.* Later when I heard Otis Redding, it was the same thing.

These people had taken gospel music and crossed that corner from gospel to pop.

Piano Pop/Gospel–Use of Raised 9 Chord

⑯ "Drown In My Own Tears"

This song could be done in any church in any way you want. But it's still the blues, a real churchy blues. And it's also a pop song and a hit record. To me it was an anthem for people like Sister Rosetta Thorpe and so many great people who over the years were misunderstood because they had taken on some new territory with music that crossed over barriers. At one time, the church was the church and the blues was the blues. But now it's all music.

In some people's minds, "never the twain shall meet" and "never the train shall cross the tracks" and all of that. But in my mind, whether I'm playing in a church or if I'm playing in a juke joint, it's the same thing to me as music. And it's either good or bad.

The Famous Lick

🎵 "The Famous Lick"

A lot of people say to me, "Doc, how do you play the famous lick?" Well, I didn't know what the "famous lick" was until some guys sat down at the piano and I figured out that the lick that they were speaking of was this:

It's a very simple lick. It's a sound more than anything.

Basically, to me, there are many "famous licks." That lick came out of so many boogies.

If I heard Huey "Piano" Smith play a lick, he might play:

Huey Smith Lick

Or if Allen Toussaint played it, he might play:

Allen Toussaint Lick

Or if I heard Fats Domino play the same lick, he might play:

Fats Domino Lick

Or if I heard James Booker play the lick he might play:

James Booker Lick

Or if I heard Lloyd Glenn play it, he might play something like:

Lloyd Glenn Lick

In other words, each piano player plays something in his own given style. the one guy who would always do something different was Professor Longhair, who might play the same lick like:

Professor Longhair Lick

That was Professor Longhair's contribution to the "famous lick." The point is, there's a lot of "famous licks."

Styles

🔢 Clarence "Pine Top" Smith

When "Pine Top" Smith did the "Pine Top Boogie," his style was totally unique in its time, totally different from the other boogie pianists.

Pine Top Boogie: Introduction

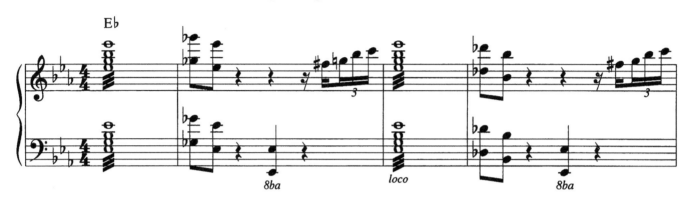

Pine Top Boogie: Components

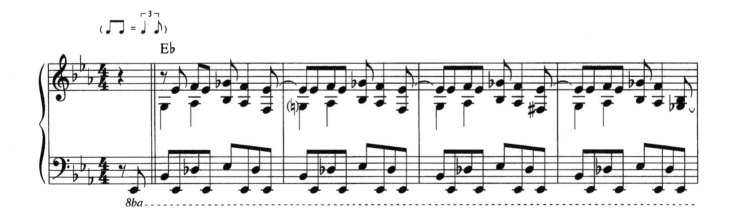

19 Albert Ammons

The great Albert Ammons played this kind of Boogie:

Albert Ammons Type Boogie

◆20 Jimmy "Papa" Yancey

Jimmy "Papa" Yancey played a different kind of boogie thing. Listen to the recorded example. He had a much fuller left hand. There's a different texture to the bass.

Huey "Piano" Smith took all of these sounds and he simplified it to where he would play something like the recorded example.

He made a rhythm pattern that was an offshoot of what Fats Domino played. (Listen to the recorded example.)

He took that and make it a real rolling, full sound.

21 Jelly Roll Morton

All of the guys had rolling styles of piano playing. There was the old, old style of guys like Jelly Roll Morton.

22 Huey Smith

Huey Smith did the country type of rolling thing.

That was on Smiley Lewis' record of "I Hear You Knocking" and a lot of other records.

23 Fats Domino

Fats Domino's rolling technique was like:

24 Rolling Styles

All of the styles of rolling are based on a trilling or tremolo sort of thing:

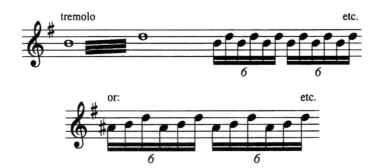

The idea of the trilling is basically a way of making a piano solo stand out from another part of the song.

A lot of guys who sing and play use this as a way to play off of their singing. That's why I was singing a Buddy Bolden song by Jelly Roll, because Jelly Roll had this really beautiful ability to make these luscious trills which he'd use in between his vocal to give himself some pitch notes. That's part of the charm of the usage of the rolling sound.

But there's a much further style of this. When Fats Domino played on the Lloyd Price record of "Lawdy Miss Clawdy," he played something like the recorded example.

He started rolling with both hands. Until then I hadn't heard anybody do that full a sound with the rolling. It was always basically one hand or the other. That kind of set a precedent for real rich bottom sound on piano with the advent of the electric bass. Prior to that you couldn't do that much bottom on the piano without muddying up the upright bass. Nowadays, we accept these things as part of the music, but at one time it just wasn't done because there weren't facilities to record it.

◈25 Various Styles, Same Piece of Music

I'll give some examples of the styles of various guys playing the same kind of piece.

◈26 Allen Toussaint

First, take the sound that Allen Toussaint came up with.

Allen Toussaint

2nd Chorus

◆27 Huey Smith

The way Huey Smith would've played is different. One of the things Huey did was to play discordant things on the V chord.

When he played "I Hear You Knocking" he used the whole tone scale:

Things like that were very unique.

◆28 Professor Longhair

Professor Longhair would've played the same pattern differently. (Listen to the recorded example.)

◆29 Toots Washington

Toots Washington's style was based on the old 8-bar blues style.

◆30 Champion Jack Dupree

Champion Jack Dupree or another of the more gut-bucket players would've played the same thing like the recorded example. Jack's style is much more "pre-historic."

◆31 Archibald

A guy like Archibald (Leon T. Gross) would've played the same thing like the recorded example.

His style was much more varied than Champion Jack's.

◆32 Junket Style

This is what we call the "Motor Junket Blues" style.

Motor Junket Blues

That's a typical style.

⟨33⟩ Jolly Landrey/"Wild Chapatulas"

Guys like Jolly Landrey from the Wild Chapatulas played the same thing in this style. (Listen to the recorded example.)

⟨34⟩ James Booker

As you can see, there are so many, many styles.

The way james Booker did it, he took an 8-bar blues and wrote an arrangement around it that went something like this:

James Booker Blues

8 Bar

He took the melody:

and composed a progression of chords descending chromatically:

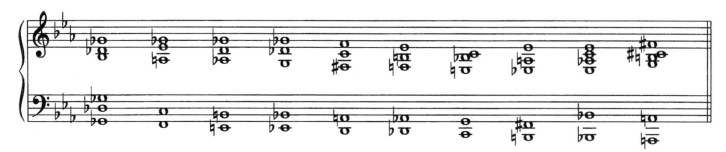

And then, when he recorded it, he added horns moving in a circle of fourths:

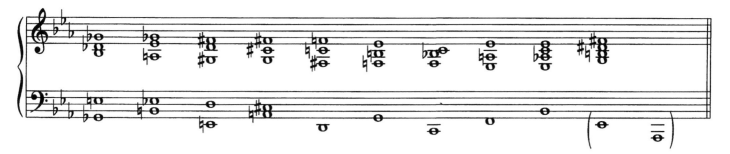

That shows you some of the things you can do with a simple structure.

No matter who plays something, they'll make it their own. This is one of the values of people picking up little things they hear, picking little things out of the air.

I'd advise every player to listen to as many people as they can.

Analysis

35 "Louisiana Lullabye"

This is a little thing called "Louisiana Lullabye."

Louisiana Lullabye

2nd Chorus

I wrote this little tune back in '57. It's a nice tune for you to build up your chops with walking bass, double-time bass and stop-time, all in one piece.

36 "Qualified"

This is a piece called "Qualified." Even though I'm going to sing a little bit, this is to show how the comp on the piano lays and how it's structured rhythmically.

The intro is a variation on a turnaround:

Qualified

Intro

If you play the comp figure long enough, it'll feel good to you because it's a funk figure. If you feel the rhythm in it, you'll notice that a lot of boogie figures come into mind.

This is a New Orleans funk rhythm, *ala* James Booker, Allen Toussaint, Dr. John, Professor Longhair and the whole bunch.

Components of Qualified

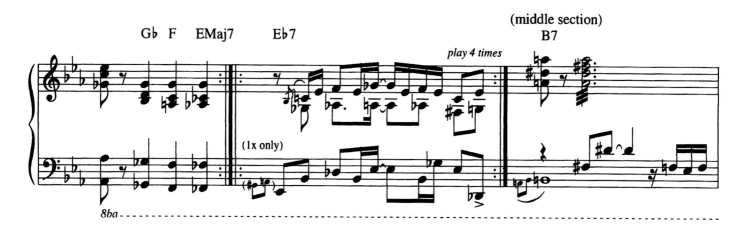

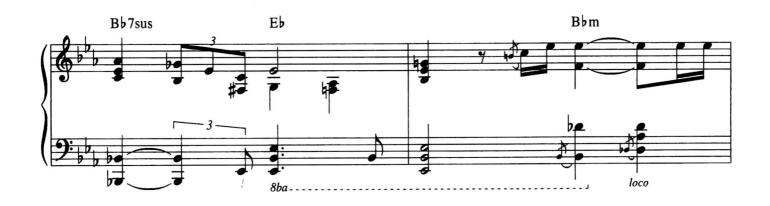

And that little turnaround going back to the root chord was:

The bridge is felt in cut-time. When we get back to the intro, we're back in funk time.

You can play this *ad infinitum*.

◆37 Ending Talk

- It's a good thing to force yourself, not only to play things in different bags and different styles, but to play them in different keys.

- Force your mind to work.

- Force yourself out of clichés and out of getting into ruts.

- The easiest thing to do when you learn something in music, is to depend on what you've learned to get yourself out of jams. But sometimes, it may be better to make a mistake and to make another mistake until you find where it leads to.

- Keep yourself playing things *fresh* in order to improve your musicianship.

Well, I hope you've gotten something out of this little radiating the 88's styles. And if you have got anything worthwhile, even if there's something you don't dig about it, you can write to me, Dr. John the Night Tripper, c/o Homespun Tapes.

I appreciate hearing from you and maybe I'll learn something from you and maybe you'll learn something further from me.

I hope you've enjoyed it as much as I have.